Primary Sources of Colonial America

Colonial Interactions with Native Americans

Cathleen Small

Cavendish
Square
New York

Published in 2018 by Cavendish Square Publishing, LLC
243 5th Avenue, Suite 136, New York, NY 10016

Library of Congress Cataloging-in-Publication Data

Names: Small, Cathleen.
Title: Colonial interactions with Native Americans / Cathleen Small.
Description: New York : Cavendish Square, 2018. | Series: Primary sources of colonial America | Includes bibliographical references and index. | Audience: Grades 6-10.
Identifiers:ISBN 9781502631343 (library bound) | ISBN 9781502634610 (pbk.) | ISBN 9781502631350 (ebook)
Subjects: LCSH: United States--History--Colonial period, ca. 1600-1775--Juvenile literature. | Indians of North America--Juvenile literature.
Classification: LCC E188.S63 2018 | DDC 973.3--dc23

Editorial Director: David McNamara
Editor: Fletcher Doyle
Copy Editor: Rebecca Rohan
Associate Art Director: Amy Greenan
Designer: Lindsey Auten
Production Coordinator: Karol Szymczuk
Photo Research: J8 Media

Printed in the United States of America

CONTENTS

Cultural Differences

The American colonists originally left England and other parts of Europe seeking a new life in a new land. They came for different reasons—some were fleeing religious persecution, others were looking for a better life in a new land or for great wealth. The journey was long, and many died en route. However, for those who survived the ocean crossing, there was the promise of a new future.

Those colonists who survived the trans-Atlantic journey encountered Native American tribes that had cultures they didn't understand. Subsequent efforts at communication between the various settlements of colonists and the numerous Native American tribes ranged from successful to violent.

How any given scenario played out depended largely on the politics and cultures of the people involved, as well as the perceived goals of both. When they could work together and establish mutually beneficial trade, interactions could be largely positive. In many cases, Native Americans taught

In the 1650s, Dutch colonists build a stockade in what is now Manhattan. It became Wall Street.

colonists skills such as farming techniques for the land, and they supplied them with food in trade for goods. In return, the colonists taught the Native Americans how to use firearms and sometimes supplied them with guns and ammunition in trade for food and support. These relationships were mutually beneficial for Native Americans and colonists. But at other times, Native Americans perceived that colonists were attempting to take over the land they lived on, and in those cases things could—and did—get violent.

Certainly, there were communication challenges. The colonists generally spoke English, French, Spanish, or Dutch. Native Americans spoke dialects from several language families. None of these language families had any similarities to European languages. The two groups had to attempt to communicate without using a common language, which was challenging at best. At times, there were interpreters who could help, such as Squanto, who helped the Pilgrims of the Plymouth colony communicate with the neighboring tribes. But many times the groups had to do their best without a common language.

There were differences in **ideology**, also. Colonists came to the New World with the idea of owning land and staking their claim, whereas Native Americans didn't have a legal, formalized system of land ownership. Some tribes didn't believe at all in land ownership, and other tribes had an informal system of residency. In either case, the beliefs surrounding land ownership didn't match up with the colonists' visions.

Religious differences were an issue, too, with colonists wishing to convert Native Americans to Christianity, and some Native Americans not interested in giving up their own markedly different spiritual beliefs. There were Native Americans who famously converted to Christianity, but for the most part the cultural differences between the natives and the Europeans were never bridged. For this, the Native Americans have suffered.

Tensions between Britain and France, and then between the British colonists and Great Britain, also affected colonists' interactions with Native Americans. The tribes eventually had to choose sides. Many chose to side with the French, and then with the British crown, causing tension, distrust, and bloodshed with the colonists.

With numerous factors contributing to it, the backdrop of colonial North America was the setting for numerous and varied experiences that ultimately helped determine the interaction between Native Americans and other US citizens today.

Early missionaries such as John Eliot preached Christianity to Native Americans. Eliot translated the Bible into a Native language and it was published in 1663.

CHAPTER
ONE

Initial Impressions

W hen European explorers first reached America, many didn't know what to expect. Explorer Christopher Columbus and the Spanish initially thought the new land was part of Asia, but eventually the Spanish realized their error. The Native Americans, with their religions and cultures so different from that of the explorers, were viewed with curiosity—and often with fear. Some viewed them as savages—and indeed, the customs of some tribes were more savage than others. There were peace-desiring tribes and tribes that wished to drive the Europeans off the land.

In some cases, alliances were formed between Europeans and natives. In other cases, there was bloodshed. And in

Chief Massasoit of the Wampanoag facilitated peaceful relationships with the Pilgrims at Plymouth Plantation.

Landing at Hispaniola in 1492, Christopher Columbus and his crew met local natives whom his crew mistook for people from the East Indies.

nearly every case, there was some level of tension as these different groups of people struggled to understand each other.

In the Beginning

Columbus's voyage across the Atlantic Ocean under the Spanish flag marks the beginning of the Colonial period in North America, even though he never landed on what would become US soil. On his first voyage, he landed in Cuba and Hispaniola [Haiti and the Dominican Republic], southeast of Florida. In three subsequent voyages, he reached ports in South America, Central America, and the Bahamas. All four of these voyages were sponsored by Spain.

Columbus always claimed the lands he visited were part of Asia, and that the native peoples he encountered were Indians (people from the East Indies, which was his target destination).

However, what Columbus found was enough to spark the interest of Europeans who saw the potential for economic and trade opportunities in the region.

The New World's Namesake

Amerigo Vespucci explored the eastern coast of what is now South America in several voyages sponsored by Portugal between 1499 and 1502. He proved Columbus had not reached Asia. German **cartographer** Martin Waldseemüller labeled the continent explored by Vespucci as America on a 1507 world map he created.

But Vespucci explored territory far south of where European colonists would eventually settle. Other explorers of the time can be credited with discovering what is now North America. One such explorer is John Cabot, an Italian explorer who is credited with helming the first European exploration of North America since the Vikings. (The Vikings are believed to have created short-lived settlements in North America in the eleventh century, but they did not colonize them.)

North American Voyager

Cabot's voyage was sponsored by King Henry VII of England. He is thought to have explored the eastern coast of Canada, in the region of Newfoundland. Cabot sailed from Bristol, England, and a 1565 **chronicle** entry for the city of Bristol claims Cabot's discovery of North America:

> This year, on St. John the Baptist's Day [June 24, 1497], the land of America was found by the Merchants of Bristow in a shippe of Bristowe, called the *Mathew*; the which said the ship departed from the port of Bristowe, the second day of May, and came home again on the 6th of August next following.

Cabot did not venture far inland. In a letter about Cabot's visit, John Day, a Bristol merchant in the Spanish trade familiar with Cabot's voyage, wrote to a Spanish Lord Grand Admiral (thought to be Christopher Columbus) in the winter of 1497–1498:

> Your Lordship will know that [Cabot] landed at only one spot of the mainland, near the place where land was first sighted, and they disembarked there with a crucifix and raised banners with the arms of the Holy Father and those of the King of England.

Day went on to describe what Cabot had seen, as relayed to him:

> They found tall trees of the kind masts are made, and other smaller trees, and the country is very rich in grass. In that particular spot, as I told your Lordship, they found a trail that went inland, they saw a site where a fire had been made, they

DISCOVERY OF NORTH AMERICA BY JOHN AND SEBASTIAN CABOT

John Cabot landed in 1497, reportedly somewhere on the eastern coast of what is now Canada.

saw manure of animals which they thought to be farm animals, and they saw a stick half a yard long pierced at both ends, carved and painted with brazil, and by such signs they believe the land to be inhabited. Since [Cabot] was with just a few people, he did not dare advance inland beyond the shooting distance of a crossbow, and after taking in fresh water he returned to his ship.

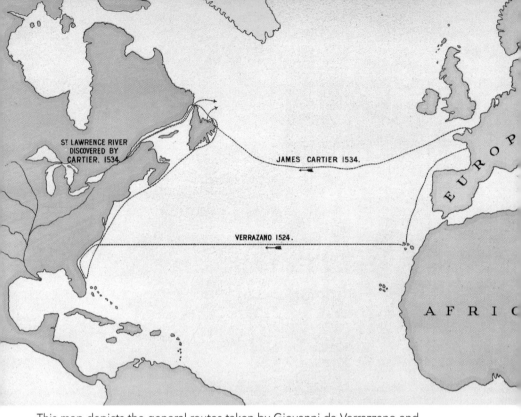

This map depicts the general routes taken by Giovanni da Verrazzano and Jacques Cartier, in 1524 and 1534, respectively.

French Exploration of the New World

Another Italian explorer, Giovanni da Verrazzano, explored North America under the sponsorship of France. Around 1508, he explored a similar region to Cabot—around the area of Newfoundland—on a ship captained by Thomas Aubert. And in 1524, Verrazzano explored the East Coast from Florida to New Brunswick (Canada). Notably, on this expedition he explored both New York Bay and Narragansett Bay (bordered by modern-day Rhode Island and Massachusetts).

Verrazzano's explorations are notable because, unlike Cabot, he actually made contact with Native Americans. While exploring New York Bay, he and his crew met members

King Philip's War brought forth numerous bloody confrontations between settlers and Native Americans.

of the Lenape tribe, and in Narragansett Bay, he and his crew met members of the Wampanoag and Narragansett tribes.

At the time Verrazzano explored the region, there were thought to be about twelve thousand Wampanoag living in forty villages in the area, comprising sixty-seven tribes and bands that collectively made up the Wampanoag Nation. However, by the time Pilgrims arrived in the region in 1620, three epidemics had reduced the number of Wampanoag to fewer than two thousand. One particular band of Wampanoag formed an alliance with the Pilgrims when they arrived, because their leader, Sachem Massasoit, believed the Pilgrims could be an ally if the dwindling bands and tribes of the Wampanoag were attacked by the Narragansett. In return, the Wampanoag, along with the Samoset and Tisquantum tribes, would teach the Pilgrims how to survive in the region.

This alliance existed until the 1660s, when escalating tensions caused by cultural and environmental differences resulted in a break between the Native Americans in the region and the English settlers, ultimately leading to the bloody **King Philip's War**.

The Pilgrims may have formed an alliance with the Wampanoag, but their first meetings with Native Americans weren't friendly. *Mourt's Relation*, which was written by

William Bradford and Edward Winslow and first printed in 1622, describes an early-morning meeting between the Pilgrims and Native Americans in the region:

> One of our company, being abroad, came running in, and cried, "They are men! Indians! Indians!" and withal their arrows came flying amongst us. Our men ran out with all speed to recover their arms; as by the good providence of God they did … The cry of our enemies was dreadful, especially when our men ran out to recover their arms … Our men were no sooner come to their arms, but the enemy was ready to assault them.

The Pilgrims succeeded in fighting off the Native Americans, with the book relating:

> Thus it pleased God to vanquish our enemies and give us deliverance. By their noise we could not guess that they were less than thirty or forty, though some thought that they were many more. Yet, in the dark of the morning, we could not so well discern them among the trees, as they could see us by our fire-side.

Interestingly enough, *Mourt's Relation* was thought to have been used to encourage others to come to the New World, though the detailed description of the Pilgrims' early interactions with Native Americans may not have been much of a lure!

Native American Accounts of Early Colonists

Tensions between Native Americans and colonists arose for a number of reasons. There were cultural differences, of course. The early colonists were strong in their Christian faith, and many wanted to convert Native Americans to Christianity. The English brought **Calvinist** Protestantism, and the

French brought Catholicism. Native Americans had a variety of religious practices but they were not all **monotheistic,** as those of Christians are. Some were **animistic, polytheistic,** or **henotheistic.**

But there were also differences in their views of nature, land, and agriculture. Colonists were used to a European tradition of land ownership, whereas native tribes did not have a formal land ownership system. As Native American law professor and scholar Rebecca Tsosie, a descendant of the Yaqui tribe, wrote in *American Indian Nations: Yesterday, Today, and Tomorrow*:

> While it is true that no Native people … maintained written land titles prior to the arrival of the Europeans, there is a rich tradition of "rights" and "responsibilities" that accompanies Native narratives about the land. In the broader sense of "ownership," Native peoples most definitely maintained political and cultural claims to their ancestral lands.

The cultural differences between the Native Americans and the early colonists caused many Native Americans to feel frustrated, as if the colonists had come to the territory and then expected Native Americans to conform to their customs. This sentiment was summed up in a short letter from a Native American from the Wicomesse tribe to the governor of Maryland, written in 1633:

> Since that you are here strangers and come into our Countrey, you should rather confine yourselves to the Customes of our Countrey, than impose yours upon us.

Some Native Americans also rebelled against the aggressive tactics they felt the early settlers used when arriving in North America, as stated in this 1609 speech by Powhatan, recorded by John Smith:

> Why will you take by force what you may obtain by love? Why will you destroy us who supply you with food? What can you get by war? We are unarmed, and willing to give you what you ask, if you come in a friendly manner …Take away your guns and swords, the cause of all our jealousy, or you may die in the same manner.

Powhatan, the chief of an alliance of Native Americans in Virginia in the early 1600s, is notable as the father of Pocahontas, who married an English settler, John Rolfe, in 1614. The marriage brought about a temporary peace between the Native Americans and colonists in the region. Powhatan believed peace was possible between the Native Americans and the colonists, and it's worth noting that his use of the word "jealousy" in his 1609 speech does not express envy, as we think of the word used today. More likely, he meant the word to express frustration, as he did not believe there was a need for weapons and violence between the colonists and the Native Americans.

One of Many Conflicts

The conflicts between the Powhatan tribes and the colonists at Jamestown were but one example of the tensions between Native Americans and colonists—but a well-known one. Similar tensions and alliances existed all along the East Coast as colonists from England and Europe streamed into this New World and began to settle on the lands that native tribes had inhabited for years.

Chief Powhatan

While Chief Powhatan generally believed that peace was possible between the colonists and the Native Americans, by no means was he a submissive ruler of the thousands of Native Americans in his tribes. Chief Powhatan ruled what is now eastern Maryland and Virginia, an area that included the Jamestown settlement. He had a complicated relationship with John Smith, who represented the colonists in Jamestown. At times he viewed Smith and the colonists as allies, and at other times he took actions that indicate his distrust or dislike of the colonists. In a 1608 discussion with John Smith on trade between the Powhatan tribes and the Jamestown colonists, Chief Powhatan had this to say:

> Yet Captaine Smith ... some doubt I have of
> your comming hither, that makes me not so
> kindly seeke to relieve you as I would: for
> many doe informe me, your comming hither
> is not for trade, but to invade my people,
> and possesse my Country.

The colonists at Jamestown saw the Powhatan tribes as somehow lesser to the colonists—in 1609, they tried to establish Chief Powhatan as a subject of King James I. The chief resisted, and when John Smith left Jamestown for England, Chief Powhatan cut off Native trade with the colonists and ordered attacks on those who left the fort at Jamestown. Due to Chief Powhatan's actions, approximately 80 percent of the colonists at Jamestown died. However, relations between the Powhatan tribes and the colonists thawed in 1614, when Powhatan's daughter, Pocahontas, married colonist John Rolfe. It was a time of constant posturing between the Powhatan tribes and the colonists. Who would be submissive to whom?

Alliances and Tensions

The early settlers all had interactions with Native Americans. Whether those interactions were hostile or friendly depended on the tribes involved and the colonies in question. In some cases, there was outright hostility. In other cases, there was a sort of tense peace between colonists and Native Americans. And in still other cases, strong alliances were formed.

To understand the complex relationships between the colonists and the Native Americans, it's helpful to understand where and how the earliest colonies were formed.

Jamestown, Virginia

The first permanent English settlement in the New World was Jamestown, Virginia. It was founded in 1607 by 104 colonists. George Percy, who was among those first settlers

On the banks of the Charles River in 1635, Native Americans greeted the Puritans. The Puritans settled after the Pilgrims.

and served two terms as the governor of Jamestown, rapturously described the colonists' first experience when they landed after five months at sea:

> The same day we entered into the Bay of Chesupioc [Chesapeake] directly, without any let or hindrance. There we landed and discovered a little way, but we could find nothing worth the speaking of, but fair meadows and goodly tall Trees, with such Fresh-waters running through the woods, as I was almost ravished at the first sight thereof.

Percy's enthusiasm did not last. He described the colonists' first experience later that same night with the region's Native Americans:

> At night, when we were going aboard, there came the Savages creeping upon all fours, from the Hills, like Bears, with their Bows in their mouths, [who] charged us very desperately in the faces, hurt Captain Gabriel Archer in both his hands, and a sailor in two places of the body very dangerous. After they had spent their Arrows, and felt the sharpness of our shot, they retired into the Woods with a great noise, and so left us.

The colonists at Jamestown initially regarded the Native Americans with fear and caution. Percy describes their assumptions when, a couple of days later, the colonists further explored the region:

> We marched some three of four miles further into the woods, where we saw great smokes of fire. We marched to those smokes and found that the Savages had been there burning down the grass, as we thought either to make their

Jamestown, the first permanent English settlement in America, is on the James River in what is now Virginia. This image is from a National Park Service painting.

plantation there, or else to give signs to bring their forces together, and so to give us battle.

Percy and the other colonists immediately assumed the Native Americans must be either staking claim to the territory or preparing for battle, but there is no verified explanation of why the Native Americans had been burning grass in the area.

Indeed, Percy describes a scene just days later, in which the Native Americans shared a meal and their customs with the colonists:

> There was a many of other Savages which directed us to their Town, where we were entertained by them very kindly ... They went into their houses and brought out mats and laid upon the ground: the chiefest of them sat

all in a rank; the meanest sort brought us such dainties as they had, and of their bread … They would not suffer us to eat unless we sat down … After we were well satisfied they gave us of their Tobacco … [and] showed us, in welcome, their manner of dancing.

Although the colonists and the Native Americans could not communicate in a common spoken language, both groups were slowly learning that the other didn't necessarily mean them harm. Tensions and alliances between the settlers at Jamestown and the native tribes from the region would ebb and flow as the colony developed, but the colonists' initial fear of the Native Americans was slowly changing.

It's difficult to know what the Native Americans' reactions to the colonists were, because written documentation from a native perspective does not exist. Some speeches of Chief Powhatan were recorded, but they were recorded by colonist John Smith, and thus are subject to his **bias**. However, based on Smith's reporting of his conversations with Chief Powhatan in 1608, it appears Powhatan was quite clear about his desire for peace with the colonists:

Captaine Smith, you may understand that I having seene the death of all my people thrice, and not any one living of these three generations but my selfe; I know the difference of Peace and Warre better than any in my Country … Let this therefore assure you of our loves, and every yeare our friendly trade shall furnish you with Corne; and now also, if you would come in friendly manner to see us, and not thus with your guns and swords as to invade your foes.

Chief Powhatan had seen three generations of his tribe destroyed by war, and he did not wish to see that happen

Pilgrims participated in religious services at Plymouth Plantation. They had come to North America seeking religious freedom, not economic gain.

again. He implored Smith to approach the Powhatan people in peace, and in turn, the Powhatan would continue to supply the colonists with corn.

Plymouth, Massachusetts

Little more than a decade after Jamestown was established, the Pilgrims sailed for the New World on the *Mayflower*, arriving in November 1620. Unlike Jamestown, which was settled by men, Plymouth was settled by families, including women and children.

Plymouth lies at the edge of Cape Cod Bay, south of what is now Boston, Massachusetts. John Smith had surveyed and named the region, but it wasn't settled until the Pilgrims arrived. It is considered the first colony in New England. (Jamestown is further south, in the Mid-Atlantic region.)

The Pilgrims were **separatists** who were fleeing religious persecution. Their religious beliefs were similar to those of the **Puritans**—they both followed the teaching of John Calvin—with one big exception. The Puritans wanted to cleanse the Church of England of any hint of Roman Catholicism. The Pilgrims wanted to separate completely from the Church of England.

Just as John Smith and the colonists in Jamestown had a relationship with Chief Powhatan, the Pilgrims had a relationship with the native tribes in the region. The local natives were members of the Wampanoag tribes, led by Chief Massasoit. One of these natives was Squanto, a member of the Patuxet band of Native Americans.

The Patuxet were nearly extinct by this time, with epidemics of European diseases having killed many of them. Squanto had avoided the epidemics. He acted as a go-between for the Wampanoag and the Pilgrims. He lived with the Pilgrims for nearly two years, serving as an advisor and translator.

Squanto was instrumental in the first Thanksgiving, which took place in the fall of 1621. The exact date is not known. The feast was held to celebrate a bountiful fall harvest. Only half of the Pilgrims who had sailed on the *Mayflower* had survived the first winter in Plymouth, and those fifty-three were present at the first Thanksgiving, along with approximately ninety members of the Wampanoag tribe and Chief Massasoit. The Pilgrims who attended the feast included four women and nearly twenty-five children and teenagers of both genders. It was truly a family event for the surviving Pilgrims.

The feast and festivities lasted for three days. In *Mourt's Relation,* Edward Winslow described the feast in this way:

> Our harvest being gotten in, our governor sent
> four men on fowling, that so we might have

Famously, Native Americans and Pilgrims shared a meal at the first Thanksgiving in 1621. This scene was painted by Jean Louis Gerome Ferris in 1932.

after a special manner rejoice together, after we had gathered the fruits of our labors; they four in one day killed as much fowl, as with a little help beside, served the company almost a week, at which time amongst other recreations, we exercised our arms, many of the Indians coming amongst us, and amongst the rest their greatest king Massasoit, with some ninety men, whom for three days we entertained and feasted, and they went out and killed five deer, which they brought to the plantation and bestowed on our Governor, and upon the Captain and others.

Edward Winslow and William Bradford are the only two Pilgrims known to have written about the first Thanksgiving. Bradford's description in his *Of Plimoth Plantation* largely parallels Winslow's account of the events of that time, but it

Squanto:
From Captive to Guide

The story of how Squanto survived the epidemics that wiped out the Patuxet is interesting. In 1605, Squanto was reportedly captured by a British explorer and taken to England, where he learned English and was eventually returned to the New World. However, in 1614, Squanto was abducted a second time, along with nearly thirty other Native Americans, by Englishman Thomas Hunt. Hunt intended to sell them into slavery in Spain. Squanto ultimately escaped and was eventually brought back to the New World by an associate of John Smith's. When Squanto found all the Patuxet people deceased, he went to live with the neighboring Pokanoket tribe.

Given that Englishmen had abducted Squanto twice (though some historians believe only the second abduction happened), it's surprising that Squanto ended up being an ally for the Pilgrims. He had picked up a reasonable amount of the English language, enough to act as a translator. He was also able to assist the Pilgrims in learning how to cultivate crops in the region and how to trade with local tribes. He is also thought to have facilitated the first Thanksgiving.

So valuable was Squanto to the Pilgrims that he ultimately became the center of tensions between the Pilgrims and the Pokanoket tribe, with whom the Pilgrims traded. Squanto may have been the source of some of this tension—it is reported that he knew well his value to the Pilgrims and was hungry for more power. Pilgrim Edward Window wrote in his book *Good Newes from New England*:

> [Squanto] would oft threaten the Indians, sending them word in a private manner

Squanto provided help to the Pilgrims in many areas. Here, he shows them how to use fish as fertilizer for crops.

we were intended shortly to kill them, that thereby he might get gifts for himself, to work their peace.

Squanto also reportedly spread false rumors that Chief Massasoit planned to attack the Pilgrims, which led the Wampanoag to shun Squanto. The Pilgrims were angry, too, but William Bradford, the governor of Plymouth, was so devoted to Squanto that he forgave his transgression.

includes a line that may have contributed to a modern-day Thanksgiving tradition:

> And besides water foule, ther was great store of wild Turkies, of which they tooke many, besids venison, &c. Besids, they had about a peck a meale a weeke to a person, or now since harvest, Indean corn to yt proportion. Which made many afterwards write so largly of their plenty hear to their freinds in England, which were not fained, but true reports.

Bradford would flunk a spelling test today, but his description tells us that at the time of the first Thanksgiving, the Pilgrims were hunting wild turkeys in addition to deer and **waterfowl**, and that the reports the Pilgrims sent to friends in England about the amount of food at the feast were not exaggerated.

There is actually no record of turkey having been on the menu at the first Thanksgiving, but Bradford's mention of wild turkey being hunted at that general time period has led to turkey being a staple at American tables on Thanksgiving.

There is also no record of whether the Pilgrims invited the Native Americans to the feast or whether the Native Americans simply joined them without invitation. Regardless, it is confirmed by Winslow's and Bradford's accounts that the Pilgrims and the Wampanoag did indeed share a feast together in the fall of 1621.

New Netherland

Although Jamestown and Plymouth are probably the two best-known colonies, there were others, too. The Dutch East India Company hired explorer Henry Hudson to find a passage through the New World to Asia in 1609, and shortly thereafter the Dutch began to settle and populate the area

A woodcut from DeLaet's map of 1630 shows the regions then known as New Netherland and New England.

known as New Netherland. Officially established as a colony in 1624, New Netherland included parts of New York, New Jersey, Connecticut, Pennsylvania, and Delaware.

The settlers were primarily involved in trading fur, which was plentiful in the region. That territory had been inhabited with Algonquian and Iroquois tribes, and the Algonquians became trading partners with the settlers in New Netherland. However, by the late 1620s, the Mohawks, who were part of the Iroquois Nation, had taken over much of the Native American fur trade in the region.

While the Dutch settlers were able to interact mostly peacefully with the region's Native Americans in the beginning, tensions arose over land use and ownership. The Dutch East India Company attempted to purchase the land from the Native Americans in trade, but the natives had different views on land ownership. Many of the Algonquian tribes and bands in the region were **migratory.** They would

The Hudson Bay Trade Shop was an important place for settlers involved in the fur trade to do business with Native Americans.

periodically leave and return to the land. The Dutch settlers thought they had vacated the land when they accepted the gifts the Dutch had provided in trade.

French Colonies in North America

The French were also interested in colonizing the New World, but many of their early attempts were unsuccessful. Jacques Cartier officially founded New France (located in what is now eastern Canada) in the 1530s, but subsequent early settlements in North America failed due to disease, weather problems, and attacks by other powers in the region, such as a Spanish attack that destroyed a French settlement in present-day Florida in 1565.

The French slowly began to populate the Great Lakes region and southward, but their expansion was slow. Unlike Plymouth, which had been settled by both men and women, the French colonies were mostly settled by men, who then often married Native American women. King Louis XIV did try to send women to the region, so that French settlers could marry French women, but the experiment was not a great success. However, a positive consequence of French settlers marrying Native American women was that it typically made for relatively peaceful relations between the French colonists and the native tribes in the region.

Much like the English, though, the French government hoped to convert natives in the region to Christianity—in this case to the Catholic faith. The Ordonnance of 1627, issued by Cardinal Richelieu, chief minister under King Louis XIII, stated:

> The descendants of the French who are accustomed to this country, together with all the Indians who will be brought to the knowledge of the faith and will profess it, shall be deemed and renowned [known as] natural Frenchmen.

Whether the Native Americans actually *wanted* to become "renowned natural Frenchmen" is unknown, but certainly they were generally allies to the settlers of New France. A century later, when the colonists of New France would fight against the English colonists in the French and Indian War, the far-outnumbered French would be supported by their Native American allies.

CHAPTER THREE

Interaction Turns to Conflict

As colonial settlements grew and population expanded, tensions escalated. There were still native tribes and colonial settlements that coexisted peacefully, but there were also a number of major clashes between the two groups.

Jamestown was the first colonial settlement in the New World, and it went through periods of peace and conflict with the Native Americans of the region. In the early 1600s, Chief Powhatan and John Smith facilitated a relatively calm period of alliance between Native Americans and colonists at Jamestown. The two leaders engaged in cat-and-mouse posturing in which they jockeyed for power.

By the 1670s, however, tensions were rising. A dispute between colonist Thomas Mathew and the Doeg tribe on the Potomac River led Mathew and his neighbors to kill several

The burning of Jamestown in 1676 was part of Bacon's Rebellion.

John Mason carried out the Pequot attack in 1637, in which more than six hundred Pequot were killed in what is now Connecticut.

natives who were taking his livestock. The Doeg killed one of Mathew's employees in retaliation. This led colonial militia to attack the Doeg along with the neighboring but uninvolved Susquehannock tribe. Native Americans responded by engaging in a series of attacks on colonial settlements in Virginia.

Bacon's Rebellion

The governor of Virginia, Sir William Berkeley, set forth a plan to gather Native American allies of the colonists and to isolate the Susquehannock tribe, which at this point was at the center of the conflict. However, not everyone agreed with Berkeley's plan. Among the **detractors** was Nathaniel Bacon, a member of Governor Berkeley's council.

Bacon wanted to fight the Native Americans—in part to retaliate for the attacks and in part to clear them out of the way for expansion of the colony. Bacon gathered a following and set about on his own course, persuading members of the Occaneechi tribe to attack the Susquehannock. After the Occaneechi carried out Bacon's plan, he then turned on them.

His allies killed a number of Occaneechi men, women, and children, and looted their village.

Berkeley opposed Bacon's actions and expelled him from the council. A war of sorts then erupted between Bacon and his followers, and Berkeley and his followers. At first, the feud between the two groups of colonists mostly involved **looting** of properties and other nonviolent acts. Berkeley ordered Bacon reinstated to the council but then expelled him again.

Bacon and his followers issued a document on July 30, 1676: the Declaration of the People, Against Sir William Berkeley and Present Governors of Virginia. It criticized Berkeley on many levels, including his perceived failure to protect colonists from Native American attacks, and called for his surrender:

> For having, Protected, favoured, and
> Emboldned the Indians against his Majesties
> Loyall Subjects, never Contriving, requiring,
> or appointing any due or proper meanes
> of Satisfaction for theire many Incursions,
> Murthers, and Robberies committed upon us.

Bacon and his followers continued their attacks on local native tribes, including the Pamunkey, who were an ally of the English. Berkeley tried in vain to stem the rebellion.

At one point, Berkeley temporarily fled the region but returned in time to see Bacon and his followers burn down Jamestown on September 19, 1676. Berkeley watched the fire from a distant shore, to which he had retreated.

Bacon died suddenly nearly a month after his followers burned Jamestown. The rebellion faltered after that, and by the following summer, it was over. However, there were long-lasting consequences for native and colonial interactions. The Pamunkey, Occaneechi, and Susquehannock tribes felt the sting of having been targeted by Bacon and his followers and wouldn't quickly forget. Governors following Berkeley recognized that while they

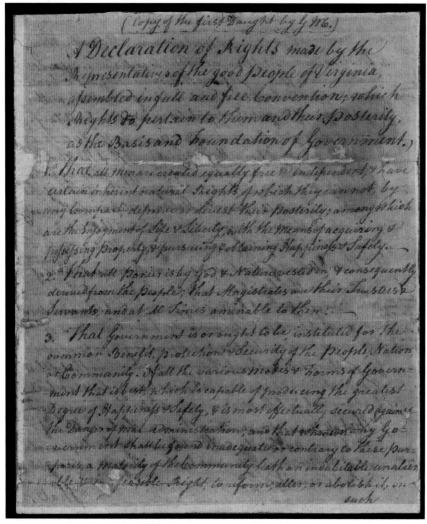

The Virginia Declaration of Rights, drafted in 1776, was a model for the Bill of Rights that was added to the United States Constitution.

might not have agreed with Bacon's tactics against the Native Americans, they *did* need to have a stronger policy on Native Americans, or they would risk a similar civil war to the one that had erupted between Bacon's followers and Berkeley **loyalists**.

King Philip's War

There was a bloody conflict going on concurrently far to the north of Jamestown, in the area that is now New England. It resulted in significant loss of life. Considering the population size in the region, some say King Philip's War, which ran from 1675 to 1676, was the bloodiest war in the history of the North American settlements. Ten percent of colonists eligible for military service were killed during the conflict, and twelve towns in the region were destroyed, with many more damaged. Native Americans from the Wampanoag and Narragansett tribes and their allies attacked more than half of the towns in New England.

Initially, the Pilgrims who settled Plymouth and surrounding towns lived peacefully with the Wampanoag, facilitated in part by relations with Wampanoag Chief Massasoit. However, when Metacom, Massasoit's second son, became chief of the Wampanoag in 1662, he took a stand against the colonists encroaching on Wampanoag territory. Metacom, also known as King Philip, was frustrated by the colonists forcing him to sign a peace treaty that required his people to surrender their guns, and by colonists hanging three members of the Wampanoag tribe for murdering another member. All of these factors led Metacom and his followers and allies to launch a series of attacks on colonial towns in the region in 1675.

Edward Randolph, a British colonial administrator who reported to the king of England, wrote about the conflict in a 1675 letter. He listed several possible causes of the fighting (including colonial attempts to convert Native Americans to Christianity) but concluded:

> Various are the reports and conjectures of the causes of the present Indian warre ... But the government of the Massachusetts ... [has] contributed much to their misfortunes, for they first taught the Indians the use of arms, and admitted them to be present at all their musters and trainings, and shewed them how to handle, mend and fix their muskets, and have been furnished with all sorts of arms by permission of the government.

Metacom, chief of the Wampanoag circa 1670, was known to settlers as King Philip of Pokanoket.

Randolph believed the colonists empowered the Native Americans by giving them guns and showing them how to use them. Not surprisingly, when the colonists later ordered the Native Americans to surrender those same guns, the natives were not pleased.

The Native Americans were eventually defeated, but not before significant damage was inflicted on colonial settlements in New England as well as to the native tribes in the region. By the time the conflict ended in 1678, more than a thousand colonists and three thousand Native Americans had been killed by disease and by bullets.

The Native American tribes underwent significant alteration as a result of King Philip's War. Some tribes were nearly eliminated and folded into other tribes, some were exiled to Bermuda, and others relocated to other parts of the region.

Colonial Interactions with Native Americans

While the colonists experienced great loss during the fourteen months of fighting, they were able to rebuild and expand their settlements across Massachusetts, Connecticut, and Rhode Island. The Native American tribes that had once inhabited those regions had been defeated, leaving the area open for colonial expansion.

The French and Indian War

Three-quarters of a century after Bacon's Rebellion and King Philip's War, the most significant conflict in the colonial period erupted. It became known in North America as the French and Indian War. Known by the British and Europeans as the Seven Years' War, the French and Indian War broke out in 1754.

Often, wars are named with respect to the opposing sides. In this case, though, the French and Indians were on the same side. They were allied against the British, their colonists, and their native partners.

The French had settled in a large region stretching roughly from the St. Lawrence River and the Great Lakes regions southward—to the west of the more coastal territories settled by the English colonists. The French had lived largely in peace with the native tribes in their region. Their main goal was trade. The French took far less land in North America, which lessened conflict with the region's Native Americans.

So, when war broke out between British and French colonists over control of the Forks of the Ohio (the **confluence** of the Alleghany and Monongahela Rivers, which formed the Ohio River), the French colonists had a lot of Native American allies to help them in their fight against the English colonists. That was good news for the French colonists, who were greatly outnumbered. The French had approximately sixty thousand colonists compared to the two million English colonists.

War was officially declared by Britain in 1756. The conflict lasted seven years after that and consisted of numerous battles. Ultimately, the losing French ceded much of their territory to

England and some to Spain (the land west of the Mississippi River and the port of New Orleans), which firmly cemented England as the colonial power in North America.

For Native Americans, the French and Indian War had a very important outcome: the Proclamation of 1763, issued by King George III of England. Before the war, private citizens and colonial governments could make deals with Native Americans to buy land, and they could travel westward and conduct trade with natives wherever they liked. This had led to dangerous situations for both colonists and Native Americans, as disagreements led to attacks by both sides.

The Proclamation of 1763 put an end to these practices and declared that Britain and not the colonists would conduct all official relations with Native Americans, and that all land west of the Appalachians was off limits to colonists. Specifically, the proclamation stated:

> It is just and reasonable, and essential to Our Interest and the Security of Our Colonies, that the several Nations or Tribes of *Indians*, with whom We are connected, and who live under Our Protection, should not be molested or disturbed in the Possession of such Parts of Our Dominions and Territories as, not having been ceded to, or purchased by Us, are reserved to them, or any of them, as their Hunting Grounds …

This meant the colonists could no longer pressure the Native Americans into giving up their lands for whatever trade or payment they were offered. The temporary document (it was in force until the Revolutionary War) wasn't foolproof—some colonists simply defied it. But it did slow the westward expansion of the colonists.

A Woman's Perspective

The colonies were often largely male-dominated, but particularly in northern settlements there were women settlers as well. One such settler, Mary Jemison, was captured by Native Americans during the French and Indian War, and she recalled years later her experience of being abducted:

> When we set off, an Indian in the forward canoe took the scalps of my former friends, strung them on a pole that he placed on his shoulder, and in that manner carried them, standing in the stern of the canoe directly before us, as we sailed down the river ... On the way we passed a Shawnee town, where I saw a number of heads, arms, legs, and other fragments of the bodies of some white people who had just been burned.

As brutal as this description is, Jemison fared well. The prisoners captured by the Native Americans were brought back to the tribe as replacements for Native lives lost. And if the prisoners were healthy and the Native family was not still deeply grieving their lost loved one, the prisoners were often treated well. Jemison recalled:

> It was my happy lot to be accepted for adoption ... I was received by the two squaws to supply the place of their brother in the family; and I was ever considered and treated by them as a real sister, the same as though I had been born of their mother.

CHAPTER FOUR

Carryover From the Colonies

C olonial interactions with Native Americans varied widely, depending on the colony and the tribe. Some tribes and colonists were able to coexist peacefully, with mutually beneficial and mutually understood trade agreements. However, there was a lot of friction between other tribes and colonists, sometimes leading to bloodshed. The relationships were definitely not one-size-fits-all, and that was reflected in future interactions between American settlers and Native Americans.

Native Americans and the Revolutionary War

Many colonists grew tired of living under British rule and longed to start an independent nation, which led to the Revolutionary War. While this war was successful for the colonists in terms of establishing the United States of America, it was not such a rousing success for Native Americans.

Some British colonists did try to establish peaceful relations with the Native Americans. General John Burgoyne is shown negotiating an alliance.

At the start of the Revolutionary War, the colonists hoped their Native American allies would assist them in their fight against the British. However, Native Americans recognized that they had much to lose if the colonists prevailed. The British had ordered the Proclamation of 1763, which strongly limited colonial expansion westward. If the colonists won the war, in theory they would be free to spread as far west as they desired, as quickly as they desired.

Many tribes were not in favor of settlers expanding westward. Chief Pontiac of the Ottawa tribe fought against British occupation. He claimed to be the "Master of Life" in a 1763 speech during which he criticized Native Americans who formed relationships with colonists:

> This land, where you live, I have made for you and not for others. How comes it that you suffer the whites on your lands? Can you not do without them? … You would do well without them. You might live wholly as you did before you knew them … As regards those who have come to trouble your country, drive them out, make war on them. I love them not, they know me not, they are my enemies and the enemies of your brothers. Send them back to the country which I made for them. There let them remain.

Although some tribes coexisted peacefully with the colonists, most were skeptical of the colonists' views on land ownership and expansion. And so, because a colonial victory could negate the Proclamation of 1763, most Native American tribes did not support colonial military efforts during the war. Tribes such as the Cherokee, Creek, and those making up the Iroquois nation strongly supported the British war effort. For example, the Mohawk tribe led four of the six established Iroquois nations in supporting the British and carrying out raids on colonists in New York and Pennsylvania in 1778 and 1779.

This was damaging to the Iroquois nation, because colonial military forces under General George Washington turned their efforts to destroying Iroquois towns and crops to weaken the tribes' support of the British. The Iroquois tribes also began to fight amongst each other, further weakening the Iroquois nation.

When the colonists won the Revolutionary War and the British ceded to them all land between the Appalachian Mountains and the Mississippi River (in addition to the lands occupied by colonial settlements along the East Coast), it was essentially a loss for the Native Americans, too. A victory for the colonists over England meant a victory over England's allies—the Native Americans.

Westward Expansion

British colonists had been in contact with Native Americans for nearly two centuries, yet they still viewed the native culture as inferior and the natives themselves as less than civilized. This lack of respect can been seen in the treatment of Native Americans by the newly minted American citizens as they expanded westward. Native tribes were continually forced off their land. Eventually, they were sent to regions where living off the land was far more difficult. The Native Americans didn't always go quietly and without a fight, but the Americans **inexorably** expanded their territory westward, taking over native lands where they saw fit.

The Indian Removal Act, signed into law by President Andrew Jackson in 1830, made it legal for Native Americans to be forced to resettle to lands west of the Mississippi, in a region deemed Indian Territory. In Jackson's 1830 message to Congress, he stated:

> It gives me pleasure to announce to Congress
> that the benevolent policy of the Government,
> steadily purposed for nearly thirty years, in relation
> to the removal of the Indians beyond the white

settlements is approaching a happy consummation … It will separate the Indians from immediate contact with settlements of whites; free them from the power of the States; enable them to pursue happiness in their own way and under their own rude institutions; will retard the progress of decay, which is lessening their numbers, and perhaps cause them, gradually, under the protection of the Government and through the influence of good counsels, to cast off their savage habits and become an interesting, civilized, and Christian community.

Jackson maintained the belief that the natives were uncivilized, but if they just adopted the ways of the whites, they might someday **assimilate**. At the end of his address, Jackson provides his rationale for the removal of Native Americans from their homelands:

Is it supposed that the wandering savage has a stronger attachment to his home than the settled, civilized Christian? … Rightly considered, the policy of the General Government toward the red man is not only liberal, but generous. He is unwilling to submit to the laws of the States and mingle with their population. To save him from this alternative, or perhaps utter annihilation, the General Government kindly offers him a new home, and proposes to pay the whole expense of his removal and settlement.

While supporters of the Indian Removal Act likely agreed with the president's message, it's a safe assumption that many Native Americans did not view the government's "kindly" offer as so kind!

The same year Jackson signed the Indian Removal Act, the people of the Choctaw Nation were forced to move west.

Eight years later, the people of the Cherokee Nation were forced to move to Indian Territory in present-day Oklahoma over what later became called the Trail of Tears. This journey resulted in the loss of thousands of Cherokee lives.

Eventually, Americans moved further and further west, and Native Americans were relocated to specific **reservations**. These reservations still exist in numerous states, and while they are part of the United States, they are also governed by tribal law. Federal law is known as the supreme law of the land for the United States, but when it comes down to policies that are governed by state law, tribal law often takes precedence in the eyes of the Supreme Court and the federal government. It's a complicated system in which reservations are recognized as "domestic dependent nations," rather than as separate states of their own. For example, Arizona is one of the United States. Within Arizona lie numerous reservations, such as the Gila River Indian Community. Residents of the Gila River Indian Community live under tribal law, but also to some extent under state law and federal law. How these laws apply to residents of the reservation depends on the particular situation and law in question. Precedence is often—but not always—granted to tribal law in matters of justice for events occurring on tribal lands.

As Native Americans were being relocated in the years following the Revolutionary War (and beyond), missionaries were still attempting to Christianize them. It was stated in the Indian Removal Act that ultimately, native "tribes and nations must perish and live only as men." If they gave up their separate cultures and beliefs, they could live as Americans under the new cultural identity that the colonists had created. Not surprisingly, Native Americans generally did not subscribe to this view. Doing so would mean changing everything: their customs, their language, their religion, their entire way of living.

And so, the more things changed, the more they stayed the same. Americans viewed Native Americans as somehow "other" and treated them with **trepidation**. If the native people were to

Liaison for US Explorers

Meriwether Lewis and William Clark are famous for their exploration of the lands of the Louisiana Purchase and beyond between 1804 and 1806, under the order of President Thomas Jefferson. Jefferson wanted Lewis and Clark to find a water route across the new territory, to establish an American presence in the newly acquired lands, to establish trade with Native American tribes, and to study the region's plant and animal life and geography.

In 1805, Shoshone woman Sacagawea joined the Lewis and Clark Expedition, along with her husband, Frenchman Toussaint Charbonneau. Sacagawea was pregnant. She delivered her son just weeks into the journey.

Sacagawea served as a **liaison** between Lewis and Clark and the numerous Native American tribes they met. Sacagawea was able to help them as an interpreter and as a **diplomat** of sorts. An expedition of white men might raise the concerns of Native tribes they came upon, but seeing a Native American woman and her child accompanying the expedition made Native chiefs more comfortable interacting with the explorers.

An August 1805 entry in Lewis's journal describes one instance in which Sacagawea served as an interpreter, while the expedition was at Travelers' Rest in Montana. It shows the condescending and paternalistic attitude whites still had toward the native people:

> The meeting of those people was really affecting, particularly between Sah cah-gar-we-ah [Sacagawea] and an Indian woman, who had been taken prisoner at the same time with her ... [We formed] a shade for the Indians to set under while we spoke to

Lewis and Clark successfully explored a large amount of territory in North America with the help of Sacagawea acting as their liaison.

them … Acordingly about 4 P.M. we called them together and through the medium of Labuish, Charbono [Charbonneau] and Sah-cah-gar-weah, we communicated to them fully the objects which had brought us into this distant part of the country, in which we took care to make them a conspicuous object of our own good wishes and the care of our government. We made them sensible of their dependance on the will of our government for every species of merchandize as well for their defence & comfort; and apprized them of the strength of our government and its friendly dispositions towards them.

Sacagawea's presence on, and contributions to, the Lewis and Clark Expedition give an example of mostly congenial relations between Natives and settlers. Meriwether Lewis was reportedly not always complimentary of Sacagawea and of Native Americans in general, but William Clark was more willing to concede the value of her contributions to their journey.

This 1993 lithograph depicts the sorrow of the Cherokee in the 1830s as they walked along the Trail of Tears.

conform to American lifestyles, settlers and Native Americans could coexist. If not, the Native Americans could live separately, under their own rules but separated from white settlers.

Native Americans Today

Today, interactions between Native Americans and white citizens are not so different as they were years ago. Although Native Americans are active in American society, there is still a sort of "separate but equal" distribution. Many Native Americans live on reservations, where poverty and alcoholism rates can be very high. The high school graduation rate is lower among Native Americans than in the general US population, as is the college graduation rate. There are grants and scholarships to encourage more Native Americans to further their education—but at the same time, their lifestyle can still be quite different from life off the reservation.

As in many areas of domestic race relations, building bridges with native populations is a long process of accepting differences and communicating effectively between different cultures. Progress has been made, but more needs to come.

Chronology

Dates in green pertain to events discussed in this volume.

April 10, 1606: King James I issues the First Virginia Charter to the Virginia Company, authorizing its leaders to establish the Virginia colony and beginning the Colonial period.

May 13, 1607: The first permanent English colony in the New World is established at Jamestown, Virginia.

April 1614: Pocahontas, daughter of Chief Powhatan, marries colonist John Rolfe, thawing tensions between Native American tribes and the settlers in Jamestown.

September 6, 1620: The *Mayflower* leaves Plymouth, England, for North America.

November 9, 1620: The Pilgrims see land for the first time on their trip; it is Cape Cod.

December 21, 1620: The Pilgrims land in Plymouth, Massachusetts.

March 1621: Patuxet native Squanto facilitates early meetings between the Pilgrims and Native Americans in the region.

Fall 1621: The Pilgrims and the Wampanoag celebrate a fall harvest festival together in what is considered the first Thanksgiving celebration in America.

1622: The Powhatan strike at colonists around Jamestown, killing nearly 350 settlers.

May 1624: The Dutch establish the colony of New Netherland.

May 26, 1637: Allied forces of Puritans and the Mohegan slaughter residents of a Pequot village. In the Pequot War, which ended with another slaughter on July 28, the native tribe was decimated, with survivors being sold into slavery. It is the first war between Native Americans and English settlers in the northeast.

June 24, 1675: The native population attacks Swansea, Massachusetts, at the start of an attempt to wipe out the English settlers with a massive military action. This starts King Philip's War.

July 1675: Warriors from the Doeg tribe attack the Virginia plantation of Thomas Mathew. The colonists retaliate against the Doeg but also attack the innocent Susquehannock, resulting in a series of conflicts.

August 12, 1676: King Philip's War ends.

September 19, 1676: Jamestown is burned during Bacon's Rebellion; the rebellion ends the next month following the death of its leader, Nathaniel Bacon.

May 1689: King William's War, the first French and Indian War, begins with the British declaring war on France; the war ends in 1697 with the Treaty of Ryswick.

May 4, 1702: Queen Anne's War, the second French and Indian War, begins; it ends in 1713 with France ceding Newfoundland and Nova Scotia to Britain.

February 29, 1704: French and Indian forces kill fifty residents and take more than one hundred captives in a raid on Deerfield, Massachusetts.

May 28, 1754: Troops representing France and Great Britain and their Native Americans allies battle at Fort Duquesne in a struggle for control of the Ohio River Valley. This is the first fighting in what becomes the Seven Years' War, otherwise known as the French and Indian War.

May 15, 1756: Britain declares war on France, officially starting the French and Indian War.

September 13, 1759: British forces capture Quebec City in the climactic battle of the French and Indian War; the leaders of both armies, General Louis-Joseph de Montcalm of the French and Commander James Wolfe of the British, die in the fighting.

February 10, 1763: The signing of the Treaty of Paris ends the French and Indian War. This closes the Colonial period.

April 27, 1763: Chief Pontiac of the Ottawa holds a war council with chiefs and warriors of other tribes on the River Ecorse (now Council Point). They form a confederacy that attacks British forts but fails to capture major forts at Detroit and Pitt. The conflict is called Pontiac's Rebellion.

October 7, 1763: King George III issues the Proclamation of 1763, which forbids colonial expansion west of the Appalachian Mountains.

April 19, 1775: The battles of Lexington and Concord mark the start of fighting in the Revolutionary War. The war divided the Native Americans, and caused a civil war among the Six Nations of the Iroquois.

November 1804: Sacagawea joins the Lewis and Clark Expedition, acting as a diplomat and liaison for the expedition on their exploration of western territories.

Glossary

animistic A religious system that believes plants, inanimate objects, and natural phenomena have a soul.

assimilate To integrate into a larger society or culture and become more like that larger group.

bias Prejudice for or against a thing, person, or group.

Calvinist A Protestant belief system following the teaching of John Calvin and his successors. Among them are the primacy of the grace of God in man's (both men and women) salvation and God's predestination of those who will be saved and those who won't.

cartographer A person who creates maps.

chronicle A written account of historical events.

confluence The junction of two rivers that become one river.

detractor A person who doesn't believe something and speaks negatively of it.

diplomat A person able to interact with others in a sensitive way. It usually refers to someone who represents a country.

henotheistic A religious system that follows one particular god out of several.

ideology A belief system or a system of ideas.

inexorably In a way that can't be prevented.

King Philip's War A conflict that erupted in 1675 and lasted until 1676 between Native Americans in New England

and English colonists in the region (along with their Native American allies).

liaison A person who facilitates communication between groups of people.

looting Stealing goods during a war or a riot.

loyalist A person who is loyal to a specific ruler or government, particularly during times of revolt. Loyalists in Colonial America backed the British government.

migratory People or animals who move from place to place, usually depending on the season.

monotheistic A religious system that believes in a single god.

polytheistic A religious system that believes in and worships multiple gods.

Puritan An English Protestant from the late sixteenth and seventeenth centuries who wished to simplify and regulate worship within the Church of England.

reservation In this context, an area of land set aside for Native Americans.

separatist A person in favor of the separation of a group of people from a larger group. The Pilgrims wanted to separate from the Church of England, an act that was considered treasonous in Britain.

trepidation Fear or nervousness about a possible future event or action.

waterfowl Ducks, geese, and other large aquatic birds.

Further Information

Books

Frazier, Neta Lohnes. *Path to the Pacific: The Story of Sacagawea*. London: Young Voyageur, 2016.

Hale, Anna W. *The Mayflower People: Triumphs & Tragedies*. New York: Roberts Rinehart, 1995.

Hollar, Sherman. *Biographies of Colonial America: Sir Walter Raleigh, Powhatan, Phillis Wheatley, and More*. New York: Rosen Publishing Group, 2012.

Poolos, J. *The Mayflower: A Primary Source History of the Pilgrims' Journey to the New World*. New York: Rosen Central, 2004.

Smith-Llera, Danielle. *The Powhatan: The Past and Present of Virginia's First Tribes*. North Mankato, MN: Capstone, 2016.

Websites

Gilder Lehrman Institute of American History
https://www.gilderlehrman.org

This website has a wealth of resources about events in American history.

Library of Congress—Primary Source Sets
http://www.loc.gov/teachers/classroommaterials/primarysourcesets

The Library of Congress offers numerous primary sources and other resources for historical research.

Smithsonian Source
http://www.smithsoniansource.org

An excellent website for exploring primary sources supporting historical topics.

Bibliography

Books

Bradford, William. *Of Plimoth Plantation*. New York: McGraw-Hill Education, February 1981 reprint.

Drake, James David. *King Philip's War: Civil War in New England, 1675-1676*. Amherst, MA: The University of Massachusetts Press, 2000.

Percy, George, Lyon Gardner Tyler, ed. *Narratives of Early Virginia, 1606-1625*. New York: Charles Scribner's Sons, 1959 reprint.

Smith, John. *The Generall Historie of Virginia, New England, & the Summer Isles*. Glasgow, UK: James MacLehose and Sons, 1907.

Tsosie, Rebecca. "How the Land Was Taken: The Legacy of the Lewis and Clark Expedition for Native Nations." In *American Indian Nations: Yesterday, Today, and Tomorrow*. Edited by George Horse Capture, Duane Champagne, and Chandler C. Jackson. Plymouth, UK: AltaMira Press, 2007.

Weare, G.E. *Cabot's Discovery of North America*. Miami: HardPress Publishing, 2013.

Winslow, Edward. *Good Newes from New England*. Carlisle, MA: Applewood Books, 1996.

Winslow, Edward, and William Bradford, Lyon Sherman, Ed. *The Cape Cod Journal of the Pilgrim Fathers*. Reprinted from *Mourt's Relation*. East Aurora, NY: The Roycrofters, 1920.

Online Articles

Vigneras, L. A. "*The Cape Breton Landfall: 1494 or 1497. Note on a Letter From John Day.*" *Canadian Historical Review* (University of Toronto) 38, no. 3 (Sept. 1957). http://www.utpjournals.press/doi/abs/10.3138/CHR-038-03-03.

"Entry in Meriwether Lewis' journal. August 17, 1805." Journals of the Lewis & Clark Expedition. University of Nebraska. Accessed April 20, 2017. https://lewisandclarkjournals.unl.edu/item/lc.jrn.1805-08-17.

"Indian Removal Act—1830." American Indian Relief Council. Accessed April 20, 2017. http://www.nativepartnership.org/site/PageServer?pagename=airc_hist_indianremovalact.

"King George III: A Proclamation, 1763." The Gilder Lehrman Institute of American History. Accessed April 20, 2017. https://www.gilderlehrman.org/sites/default/files/inline-pdfs/t-05214.pdf.

"Mary Jemison Recalling, in 1824, Her Capture by Indians During the French and Indian War." Smithsonian Source. Accessed April 20, 2017. http://www.smithsoniansource.org/display/primarysource/viewdetails.aspx?PrimarySourceId=1197.

"Nathaniel Bacon's Declaration of Grievances." EncyclopediaVirginia.org. Accessed April 20, 2017. http://www.encyclopediavirginia.org/media_player?mets_filename=evm00002991mets.xml.

"Pontiac, an Ottawa Chief, Voicing the Proclamations of the 'Master of Life,' 1753." Smithsonian Source. Accessed April 20, 2017. http://www.smithsoniansource.org/display/primarysource/viewdetails.aspx?TopicId=&PrimarySourceId=1186.

"President Andrew Jackson's Message to Congress 'On Indian Removal' (1830)" December 6, 1830; Records of the United States Senate, 1789-1990; Record Group 46; Records of the United States Senate, 1789-1990; National Archives. Accessed April 20, 2017. https://www.ourdocuments.gov/doc.php?flash=true&doc=25.

Randolph, Edward. "Edward Randolph's Report of King Philip's War in New England, 1675." Accessed April 20, 2017. http://www.smithsoniansource.org/display/primarysource/viewdetails.aspx?PrimarySourceId=1175.

"Speech by Powhatan, as Recorded by John Smith, 1609." Smithsonian Source. Accessed April 20, 2017. http://www.smithsoniansource.org/display/primarysource/viewdetails.aspx?TopicId=&PrimarySourceId=1170.

"A Wicomesse Indian to the Governor of Maryland, 1633." Smithsonian Source. Accessed April 20, 2017. http://www.smithsoniansource.org/display/primarysource/viewdetails.aspx?TopicId=&PrimarySourceId=1172.

World Heritage Encyclopedia. "French Colonization of the Americas." Project Gutenberg Self Publishing Press. Accessed April 20, 2017. http://self.gutenberg.org/articles/eng/French_colonization_of_the_Americas.

Index

About the Author

CATHLEEN SMALL is an author and editor living in the San Francisco Bay Area. She has written nearly three dozen nonfiction books for students in grades three through twelve—on topics ranging from historical figures to technology to historical events. Cathleen is an avid reader and researcher who loves learning about a diverse range of topics. When she's not reading and writing, Cathleen loves to travel and do outdoor activities with her two young sons and her husband.